YOU LAUGH, I WIN!

THE ULTIMATE
TRY NOT TO LAUGH
CHALLENGE
JOKE BOOK

FAMILY EDITION

SERENA WEBSTER

D0111305

You Laugh, I Win! Game Rules

Easy Version

1. Find an opponent or split up into two teams.

2. Team 1 reads a joke to Team 2 from anywhere in the book.

3. The person reading the joke looks right at the opposing person or team and can use silly voices and funny faces if they wish.

4. If Team 2:

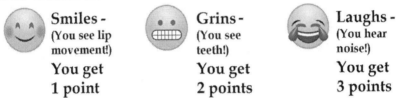

| Smiles -
(You see lip movement!)

You get
1 point | Grins -
(You see teeth!)

You get
2 points | Laughs -
(You hear noise!)

You get
3 points |

5. Read one joke at at time, then switch the giving and receiving teams.

6. The team with most points after five rounds wins! Use the score sheets on the following pages.

Challenge Version

1. Same rules apply except you get one point if you can make the other team laugh. No points for smiling or grinning.

Good luck and try not to laugh!

SCORE SHEET

	TEAM 1	TEAM 2
ROUND 1		
ROUND 2		
ROUND 3		
ROUND 4		
ROUND 5		
TOTAL		

	TEAM 1	TEAM 2
ROUND 1		
ROUND 2		
ROUND 3		
ROUND 4		
ROUND 5		
TOTAL		

	TEAM 1	TEAM 2
ROUND 1		
ROUND 2		
ROUND 3		
ROUND 4		
ROUND 5		
TOTAL		

	TEAM 1	TEAM 2
ROUND 1		
ROUND 2		
ROUND 3		
ROUND 4		
ROUND 5		
TOTAL		

	TEAM 1	TEAM 2
ROUND 1		
ROUND 2		
ROUND 3		
ROUND 4		
ROUND 5		
TOTAL		

	TEAM 1	TEAM 2
ROUND 1		
ROUND 2		
ROUND 3		
ROUND 4		
ROUND 5		
TOTAL		

	TEAM 1	TEAM 2
ROUND 1		
ROUND 2		
ROUND 3		
ROUND 4		
ROUND 5		
TOTAL		

	TEAM 1	TEAM 2
ROUND 1		
ROUND 2		
ROUND 3		
ROUND 4		
ROUND 5		
TOTAL		

SCORE SHEET

	TEAM 1	TEAM 2
ROUND 1		
ROUND 2		
ROUND 3		
ROUND 4		
ROUND 5		
TOTAL		

	TEAM 1	TEAM 2
ROUND 1		
ROUND 2		
ROUND 3		
ROUND 4		
ROUND 5		
TOTAL		

	TEAM 1	TEAM 2
ROUND 1		
ROUND 2		
ROUND 3		
ROUND 4		
ROUND 5		
TOTAL		

	TEAM 1	TEAM 2
ROUND 1		
ROUND 2		
ROUND 3		
ROUND 4		
ROUND 5		
TOTAL		

	TEAM 1	TEAM 2
ROUND 1		
ROUND 2		
ROUND 3		
ROUND 4		
ROUND 5		
TOTAL		

	TEAM 1	TEAM 2
ROUND 1		
ROUND 2		
ROUND 3		
ROUND 4		
ROUND 5		
TOTAL		

	TEAM 1	TEAM 2
ROUND 1		
ROUND 2		
ROUND 3		
ROUND 4		
ROUND 5		
TOTAL		

	TEAM 1	TEAM 2
ROUND 1		
ROUND 2		
ROUND 3		
ROUND 4		
ROUND 5		
TOTAL		

SCORE SHEET

	TEAM 1	TEAM 2
ROUND 1		
ROUND 2		
ROUND 3		
ROUND 4		
ROUND 5		
TOTAL		

	TEAM 1	TEAM 2
ROUND 1		
ROUND 2		
ROUND 3		
ROUND 4		
ROUND 5		
TOTAL		

	TEAM 1	TEAM 2
ROUND 1		
ROUND 2		
ROUND 3		
ROUND 4		
ROUND 5		
TOTAL		

	TEAM 1	TEAM 2
ROUND 1		
ROUND 2		
ROUND 3		
ROUND 4		
ROUND 5		
TOTAL		

	TEAM 1	TEAM 2
ROUND 1		
ROUND 2		
ROUND 3		
ROUND 4		
ROUND 5		
TOTAL		

	TEAM 1	TEAM 2
ROUND 1		
ROUND 2		
ROUND 3		
ROUND 4		
ROUND 5		
TOTAL		

	TEAM 1	TEAM 2
ROUND 1		
ROUND 2		
ROUND 3		
ROUND 4		
ROUND 5		
TOTAL		

	TEAM 1	TEAM 2
ROUND 1		
ROUND 2		
ROUND 3		
ROUND 4		
ROUND 5		
TOTAL		

How does one astronaut tell another astronaut that he is sorry?
He Apollo-gises!

What do you get when you cross termites and a rabbit?
Bugs Bunny!

Knock Knock!
Who's there?
Howl!
Howl who?
Howl you know unless you open the door!

What do you call a computer floating in the ocean?
A Dell Rolling in the Deep!

Where do zombies go swimming?
The Dead Sea.

Why did the spider buy a car?
So it could take it out for a spin!

Why did the cat join the Red Cross?
Because he wanted to be a first-aid kit!

Why did the bald man paint rabbits on his head? **Because from a distance they looked like hares!**

Knock, Knock!
Who's there?
Monet!
Monet who?
Monet doesn't grow on trees you know!

What do you call a horse that can't lose a race?
Sherbet!

What do you get if you cross a jogger with an apple pie?
Puff pastry!

Who is the Easter Bunny's favorite movie actor?
Rabbit De Niro!

Why was the Olympian not able to listen to music?
Because he broke the record!

What did the janitor say when he jumped out of the closet?
"SUPPLIES!"

What happened to the lost beef shipment?
Nobody's herd.

Knock, knock.
Who's there?
Canoe.
Canoe, who?
Canoe help me with my homework?

What is the name of the first electricity
detective?
Sherlock Ohms!

What do you call a fish that needs help
with his or her vocals?
Autotuna!

What do you when you make a egg
laugh?
You crack it up!

Knock, knock.
Who's there?
Wayne.
Wayne, who?
**Wayne, wayne, go away, come again
another day!**

What do you get when you cross a
hamburger with a computer?
A big mac!

Knock Knock.
Who's there?
Money.
Money who?
My knee hurts when I run!

Knock Knock!
Who's There?
Donald!
Donald who?
Donald come baby cradle in all!

Where does a detective sleep?
Under cover!

Knock Knock.
Who's there?
Amelia!
Amelia who?
Amelia an email right away!

A nickel and a dime were walking across a bridge. The nickel jumped off, but the dime didn't. Why not? **The dime had more cents.**

Knock Knock.
Who's there?
Croatia!
Croatia who?
A Croatia snack!

Knock, knock.
Who's there?
Sadie.
Sadie, who?
Sadie Pledge of Allegiance!

What do you call it when a prisoner takes his own mug shot?
A cellfie!

What do you call a pilgrim's vocabulary?
Pilgrammar!

Did you hear about the hitman who's also a janitor at the aquarium?
He sweeps with the fishes!

Why did the toilet paper roll down the hill?
He wanted to get to the bottom!

Why did the teacher marry the janitor?
Because he swept her off her feet!

What can fill a room but takes up no space?
Light!

Knock Knock.
Who's there?
Nana.
Nana who?
Nana nanna boo boo!

What happened when turtle lost his shell?
He began to feel sluggish!

What did one time bandit say to the other?
"Let's cut them off at the past!"

What has keys but doesn't open anything?
A piano!

What species of animal has the most money?
Deer, because they have the most doe!

What do you call a yak that is full of himself?
Egomani-yak!

What do you call a yak fortune teller?
Zodi-yak!

What do you do if you're attacked by mosquitoes?
Call in the S.W.A.T. team!

Why was the jester thrown in jail?
For high teasin'!

Why is Facebook like jail?
You have a profile picture, you sit around all day writing on walls!

What do you call a monkey who can't hear the telephone and who has a wife called Tang?
Who-rang-o-tang!

Why did the student give his teacher a PC?
The store was out of Apples!

Knock, knock.
Who's there?
Water.
Water, who?
Water you doing in there? Open the door, please!

Why did the chicken get a penalty?
For fowl play!

How do you get a raven to stop calling?
Take away its cell phone!

What does a football player do when he loses his eyesight?
Becomes a referee!

How do you upset a dinosaur?
Touchasaurus Spot!

What do you call a lumberjack with bad feet?
Paul Bunion!

What do they teach in witching school?
Spelling.

What material makes the best kites?
Fly paper.

Why did Julius Caesar buy crayons?
He wanted to Mark Antony!

Linda: Teacher, would you punish me for
something I didn't do?
Teacher: Of course not.
Linda: **Good, because I didn't do my
homework!**

Why is it good to stand on the service line?
Because you can order ice cream!

Did you hear about the guy who got fired from the calendar factory?
He took a day off .

What was the astronaut doing on the computer?
Looking for the space bar!

Why do dentists like potatoes?
Because they are so filling!

Did you hear the one about the Liberty Bell?
Yeah, it cracked me up!

What do you call a duck on the Fourth of July?
A fire quacker!

What is a bird's favorite Christmas story?
The Finch Who Stole Christmas!

What lies at the bottom of the ocean and twitches?
A nervous wreck!

Why are sharks so patriotic?
They are marine fish!

Who is a shark's favorite 1950s film actor?
Shark Hudson!

Why do birds fly south in the winter?
Because it's too far to walk!

A man leaves home, takes a left, another left, one more left and heads home. There are two masked men waiting there for him. Who are they?
The catcher and the umpire!

If Mississippi bought Virginia a New Jersey, what would Delaware?
Idaho... Alaska!

Why did Batman and Robin quit going fishing together?
Because Robin ate all the worms!

What do you call a protractor holding a fishing rod?
An angler!

Knock, knock.
Who's there?
Olive.
Olive, who?
Olive just around the corner!

Why did the seagull cross the beach?
To get to the other tide.

What's the hardest thing about learning
to ride a horse?
The ground!

Do you know the 16th President of the
United States?
No, we were never introduced!

What does the Statue of Liberty stand for?
Because she can't sit down!

What did one zombie say to the other?
Do you want a piece of me?

What do you say when you lose a
Nintendo game?
I want a wii-match!

What begins with E ends with E and has
one letter in it?
An envelope!

What does a cat say when somebody
steps on its tail?
Me-ow!

How deep is the frog pond?
Kneedeep, kneedeep, kneedeep!

What does the lion say to his friends
before they go out hunting for food?
'Let us prey.'

What kind of hot dog do you eat on
Halloween?
A Halloweenie!

I mustache you a question,
but I think I'll shave it for later!

How does a banker make phone calls?
On a teller-phone!

Why did the rooster cross the road?
To prove he wasn't chicken!

What do you call a bunny with oodles of money?
A billion-hare!

Why did the fish have such a huge phone bill?
Once he was on the line, he couldn't get off!

What kind of lights did Noah bring on the ark?
Floodlights!

What music note do you get if you run over an army officer with a steam roller?
A-flat major!

What's a recycling bin's favorite reading?
Litter-ature!

How do you know when it's raining cats and dogs?
When you step in a poodle!

Where do leprechauns buy their groceries?
Rainbow Foods!

Why couldn't the girl find the missing playing card?
It got lost in the shuffle!

Why do doctors make the best Jedis?
Because a Jedi must have patience!

What do you call a snowman that tells fake news?
A snow-fake!

Why do potatoes make good detectives?
Because they keep their eyes peeled!

How is a woman stranded on an island
like a woman in a department store?
They're both looking for sails!

What kind of pigs know karate?
Pork chops!

What is a Happy Farmers favorite candy?
A Jolly Rancher!

What do you get when you cross a Fedex
Driver and a UPS driver?
FED UP!

What is the cat's favorite TV show?
The evening mews!

Why'd the bowling pins stop working?
They went on strike!

Knock Knock.
Who's there?
Xavier!
Xavier who?
Xavier breath 'cause it smells real bad!

How do you make a tissue dance?
Put a boogie in it!

What did the traffic light say to the
pedestrian?
"Don't look, I'm changing!"

How did the soggy Easter Bunny dry
himself?
With a hare dryer!

Why did the computer go to the doctor?
Because it had a virus!

Where do snowmen keep their money?
In snow banks!

Why didn't the two worms go into Noah's ark in an apple?
Because everyone had to go in pairs!

What do ants eat for breakfast?
Croiss-ants!

What do you call an ant that doesn't eat cake?
Queen Ant-oinette!

Why did the egg go to the baseball game?
For the egg-stra innings!

What do spiders eat with hamburgers?
French flies!

When does a skeleton laugh?
When something tickles his funny bone!

Why was the computer shy?
Because it had hardware and software but no underware!

What powerful reptile is found in the
Sydney opera house?
The Lizard of Oz!

What did the alien say to the garden?
Take me to your weeder!

What did the nut say when it sneezed?
"Cashew!"

What do you call a goat on a mountain?
Hill Billy!

What do you call cheese that isn't yours?
"Nacho cheese!"

Did you hear about the slow swimmer?
He could only do the crawl.

When were King Arthur's army too tired to fight?
When they had lots of sleepless knights!

What kind of jewelry do rabbits wear?
14 carrot gold!

What is Captain Hooks favorite
restaurant?
Arrrrrrr-by's!

What does it do before it rains candy?
It sprinkles!

When should you take a cookie to the
doctor?
When it feels crummy!

Which reindeer has the cleanest antlers?
Comet!

What happened to the plant in math class?
It grew square roots!

What do you call a smelly fish?
A stink ray!

What do you get when you cross an Autobot with a can of paint?
Optimus Primer!

What streets do ghosts haunt?
Dead ends!

Why should you never tell a pig a secret?
Because they love to squeal!

Knock Knock.
Who's there?
Cargo.
Cargo who?
Cargo, "beep beep!"

Why did the apple cross the road?
To get to Granny Smith's house!

What do you call a dinosaur with high heels?
"My-feet-are-saurus!"

What has ears but can't hear?
A cornfield!

Knock Knock.
Who's there?
Alec!
Alec who?
"Alec-tricity. Isn't it a shock?"

How do you know when zombies are playing ice hockey?
There's a 'face-off' in the corner!

How do you know you smell bad to the police?
They shout, "Fa-breeze right there!"

What do you call a Triceratops who scores his first goal?
Dino- score!

What is a cannibal's favourite cheese?
Limb-burger!

Why did the football coach go to the bank?
To get his quarterback!

What do you call a fish with no eyes?
A Fsh!

What kind of car does a makeup artist drive?
A compact car!

What do you call the new girl at the bank?
The Nutella!

Where does a trout keep its money?
In the riverbank!

Why does a hummingbird hum?
It doesn't know the words!

Why was the ocean so embarrassed?
Everyone could see its bottom!

What happened when the house won the
door prize?
He didn't take it, he already had a door!

What do you call a moon out of its orbit?
A Luna-tic!

Knock Knock.
Who's There?
Narnia!
Narnia who?
Narnia business!

What kind of shoes can you make from banana peels?
Slippers!

What instrument does a snowboarder play?
Air Guitar!

Where do you get sandwiches in India?
At the New Delhi!

What type of stories do ships like to read?
Ferry tales!

Why shouldn't you tell a secret on a farm?
Because the potatoes have eyes and the corn has ears!

Why did the scarecrow win the award?
Because he was out standing in his field!

What do you get when you cross a robot and a tractor?
A trans-farmer!

Why is the snail the strongest animal?
Because he carries a house on his back!

How do snails make important calls?
On shell phones!

Why did the sun not go to college?
Because it already had a million degrees!

Why are environmentalists bad at playing cards?
They like to avoid the flush!

Who is the bees favorite pop group?
The Bee Gees!

What did the guitar say to the stone?
"Rock on!"

How can you tell when a clock is mad?
It will have a ticked-off look on its face!

Why do magicians do so well in school?
They're good at trick questions!

How are a mad parent and a train alike?
They both have steam coming out of their ears!

What kind of music are balloons afraid of?
Pop music!

Why does Ms. Mushroom go out with Mr. Mushroom?
Because he is a fungi!

Are mountains funny?
Yes, they're hill-arious!

What do you get when you cross a cow and a duck?
Milk and quackers!

Where do fish sleep?
In a water bed!

What do get if you cross a duck and Santa?
A Christmas Quacker!

What did the dog say to the sandpaper?
Ruff!

Why did the computer go to the doctor?
Because its megahertz!

Why don't cannibals eat clowns?
Because they taste funny!

Why are PCs like air conditioners?
They stop working properly if you open Windows!

What did mommy spider say to the teenage spider?
"You spend too much time on the web!"

Why did the boy go to the lake?
To fish for compliments!

What did the mummy movie director say
when the final scene was done?
"Ok, that's a wrap!"

What is a monster's favorite dessert?
Ghoul scout cookies!

Which is the tastiest federal building?
The U.S. Mint!

Why did the orange go blind?
It didn't have enough vitamin see!

Why did the manager hire the marsupial?
Because he was koala-fied!

Why did the boy tip-toe past the medicine cabinet?
So he wouldn't wake the sleeping pills!

Why is the football field hot after the game?
Because all the fans have left!

Why did the vegan go deep-sea fishing?
Just for the halibut!

Knock Knock.
Who's there?
Vaughan.
Vaughan who?
**You're Vaughan one sandwich short of
a picnic!**

Why was Cinderella so bad at baseball?
She had a pumpkin for a coach!

What do you call a bunny transformer?
Hop-timus Prime!

What is an aardvark's favorite pizza
topping?
Ant-chovies!

Why do sea-gulls fly over the sea?
Because if they flew over the bay they would be bagels!

Knock, knock.
Who's there?
Carl.
Carl, who?
Carl get you there faster than a bike!

How does a dog stop a video?
By pressing the paws button!

How do crazy people travel through to woods?
They take the psycho path!

How do trees get on the internet?
They log in!

Knock Knock.
Who's There?
Sarah!
Sarah who?
Sarah computer I can use?

What do you get when you have two
pinion nuts in one hand and one pinion
nut in the other?
A difference of a pinion!

Why did the deer need braces?
He had buck teeth!

Why did the vampire read the New York Times?
He heard it had great circulation!

Where do math teachers go on vacation?
To Times Square!

What do you call a nervous javelin thrower?
Shakespeare!

Two cows are standing in a field. One cow says to the other, "Are you worried about mad cow disease?" The other one says, "No, it doesn't worry me. **I'm a helicopter!"**

Knock Knock.
Who's there?
Doris!
Doris who?
Doris locked that's why I am knocking!

Why was Cinderella so very bad at
basketball?
**Because she was always running away
from the ball and kept losing her
shoes!**

How does a man on a moon get his
haircut?
Eclipse it!

What's it called when a zobie has trouble
with his house?
A grave problem!

What does a cat go to sleep on?
A caterpillow!

Did you hear about the cheese that failed
to medal at the Olympics?
It fell at the final curdle!

What do you call a cow when it is in
trouble?
Grounded beef!

What do you call a South American girl
who is always in a hurry?
Urgent Tina!

Where does Count Dracula usually eat his lunch?
In the casketeria!

Did the shark who was raised by a whale receive any education?
Yes, he was home-schooled!

Why was the Pharoah boastful?
Because he Sphinx he's the best!

What did the girl melon say when the boy melon proposed?
"We're too young. We cantaloupe!"

Why did the rooster cross the road?
To cockadoodle dooo something!

What does a dog do that a man steps into?
Pants!

What kind of car does a Jedi drive?
A Toy Yoda!

What do you call a slobby hippo?
A hippopota-mess!

Why did the sailor bring a bar of soap with him when his ship sank?
Because he thought he would wash to shore!

Why do fireflies like the rainstorms?
Because they are lightning bugs!

How do you make a firefly happy?
Cut off its tail and it will be de-lighted!

Where do belly buttons go to college?
The U.S. Navel Academy!

Why did the chicken cross the basketball court?
He heard the referee calling fowls!

What do snowmen like to eat for breakfast?
Snowflakes.

What does the papa ghost say to his family when driving?
Fasten your sheet belts!

What happens after you eat an entire gallon of "All Natural" ice cream?
You get Breyer's remorse!

What do you call a horse that lives next door?
A neigh-bor!

What do you call an exploding ape?
A ba-BOOM!.

How do you catch a squirrel?
Climb up a tree and act like a nut!

What's the difference between Santa's reindeer and a knight?
One slays the dragon, and the other's draggin' the sleigh!

Why was the cat sitting on the computer?
To keep an eye on the mouse!

Why did the orange go to the hospital?
Because it wasn't peeling well!

Knock, knock.
Who's there?
Who.
Who, who?
Is there an echo in here?

What do aliens serve their food on?
Flying saucers!

How do you throw a party for an alien?
You have to plan-et!

What does bread do after it's done baking?
Loaf around.

What do snakes do after fights?
They hiss and make up!

Why are giraffes so slow to apologize?
It takes them a long time to swallow their pride!

What do you do if you see a kidnapping?
Wake him up!

Knock, knock.
Who's there?
Panther.
Panther, who?
Panther no panths, I'm going swimming!

Where does Dorothy from OZ weigh a pie?
Somewhere over the rainbow, weigh-a-pie!

What did the daddy buffalo say to his son before it left for school?
"Bison."

What's the best tool in the ocean?
A hammerhead shark.

Have you heard the joke about the butter?
I better not tell you, it might spread.

What do you call a dinosaur with a
extensive vocabulary?
A thesaurus!

What kind of underwear do astronauts
wear?
Fruit of the Moon!

What is it called when a snowman has a temper tantrum?
A meltdown!

What did the slug say as he slipped down the wall?
My, how slime flies!

Knock Knock.
Who's there?
Pasta!
Pasta who?
Pasta la vista baby!

How do sick kangaroos get better?
They have a hop-eration!

What do you call people who are afraid of Santa Claus?
Claustrophobic.

Why did the hunter name his dog Frost?
Because Frost bites!

Did you hear about the volleyball and the iPhone that got into a fight?
The iPhone was charged and the volleyball is waiting to go to court.

Where do the pianists go for vacation?
The Florida Keys.

What does a metallic frog say?
"Rivet, rivet!"

What happens when you drop a duck
egg?
It quacks!

What superhero uses public
transportation?
Bus Lightyear!

What do you give a pumpkin who is trying
to quit smoking?
A pumpkin patch!

Why did he skeleton go to the barbecue?
To get another rib!

What position did Bruce Wayne play on
his little-league team?
He was the bat boy.

Who cleans the bottom of the ocean?
A mer-maid.

Why do dragons sleep during the day?
Because they fight knights!

What happened when the two vampires went on a blind date?
It was love at first bite!

Why did the girl put two quarters in her ear?
To hear 50 Cent!

What do you call a man with no arms and no legs on your front door step?
Matt!

What do you call a man hanging on a wall?
Art!

Knock Knock.
Who's there?
Daisy.
Daisy who?
Daisy me rollin, day hatin'!

What do you get if you cross a pig and a frog?
A ham-phibian!

What do you call a clam that doesn't share?
Shellfish!

What happens when you cross a duck and a rooster?
You get woken up at the "quack" of dawn!

Why did the birdie go to the hospital?
To get a tweetment!

.

What do you get when you cross a pig
and a cactus?
A porky-pine!

Why was the toothpick mad?
Because it was in a pickle!

How did the farmer find his lost cow?
He tractor down!

What do you give a seasick elephant?
Lots of room!

What do pigs get when they're ill?
Oinkment!

What did the carrot say when the onion
told a sad story?
"Stop! You're making me cry!"

What do you say to a hitchhiking toad?
Hop in!

Where do zombies like to go sailing?
The Dead Sea!

What do ducks have for lunch?
Soup and quackers!

What do goblins mail home while on vacation?
Ghostcards!

What's long and stylish and full of cats?
The Easter Purrade!

What do you call a grilled cheese
sandwich that's all up in your face?
Too close for comfort food!

What did the bottle of water say
to the spy?
The name's Bond....Hydrogen Bond.

What is the best season to use a
trampoline?
Spring.

What is an astronaut's worst habit?
Spacing out!

Did you hear about the guy who got hit by a can of Pepsi?
Luckily, it was a soft drink!

Why does the golfer carry two shirts?
In case he gets a hole in one!

What did the worm want to do when he grew up?
He wanted to join the Apple Corps!

What do you call a bee that lives in America?
A USB!

Why can't you work in an orange juice factory?
Because you can't concentrate!

What did the bumble bee footballer say?
Hive scored!

What do you give prisoners for dessert?
Jaily-Beans!

What did the chimney say to the other chimney?
"Stop smoking!"

Why do geese make such lousy drivers?
Because all they do is honk!

Why did the chef have to stop cooking?
He ran out of thyme!

Knock Knock!
Who's there?
Kale!
Kale who?
Obviously I have some time to kale.

Why did the bridge ask for a pen?
Because it was a drawbridge!

What is Robin Hood's favorite store?
Target!

Where do zombies like to go swimming?
The Dead Sea!

What's a cheerleader's favorite drink?
Root beer!

What do you call having your grandma on speed dial?
Instagram!

Thank you for purchasing this book. If you enjoyed it, I would really appreciate a review on Amazon. Please check out my other books in this series. Thanks for trying not to laugh!

Serena Webster

Made in the USA
Lexington, KY
15 December 2018